MINI MARVELS

SECRET INVASION

by Chris Giarrusso

MINI MARVELS
SECRET INVASION

pencils, inks, colors, lettering,
cover art, logo design & book design by
CHRIS GIARRUSSO
chrisGcomics.com

CIVIL WARDS
written by **MARC SUMERAK** *sumerak.com*

SPIDEY AND HIS AMAZING CO-WORKERS
written by **SEAN MCKEEVER** *seanmckeever.com*

LO THERE SHALL COME... A GO-CART
& ARMAGEDDON UNLEASHED
written by **PAUL TOBIN** *paultobin.net*

HULK ART CLASS, HULK SPLASH, HULK ZOO,
HULK WEB, HULK AIRPORT & HULK ICE
written by **AUDREY LOEB**

& all other stories
written by **CHRIS GIARRUSSO**

Editors: **NATHAN COSBY & WARREN SIMONS**

Collection Editor: **JENNIFER GRÜNWALD**
Editorial Assistant: **ALEX STARBUCK**
Assistant Editors: **CORY LEVINE & JOHN DENNING**
Editor, Special Projects: **MARK D. BEAZLEY**
Senior Editor, Special Projects: **JEFF YOUNGQUIST**
Senior Vice President of Sales: **DAVID GABRIEL**

Editor in Chief: **JOE QUESADA**
Publisher: **DAN BUCKLEY**

special thanks to:
JACOB CHABOT *beetlebugcomics.com*
DAVE GIARRUSSO
DREW GILL
TRACI HUI

CONSPICUOUS INVASION

written & illustrated by **CHRIS GIARRUSSO**

THE END.

CIVIL WARDS

A MINI MARVELS EVENT IN FOUR PARTS

Written by MARC SUMERAK   Illustrated by CHRIS GIARRUSSO

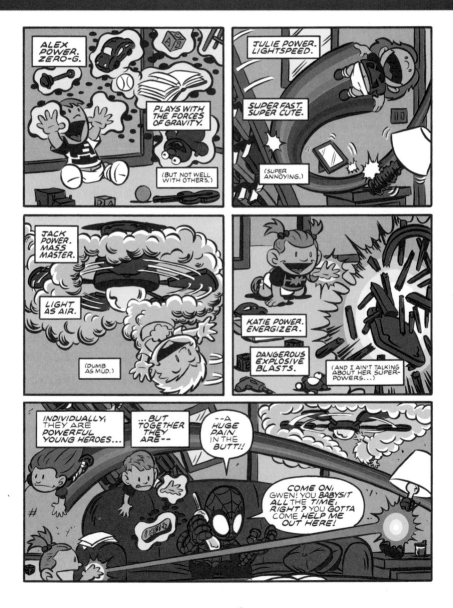

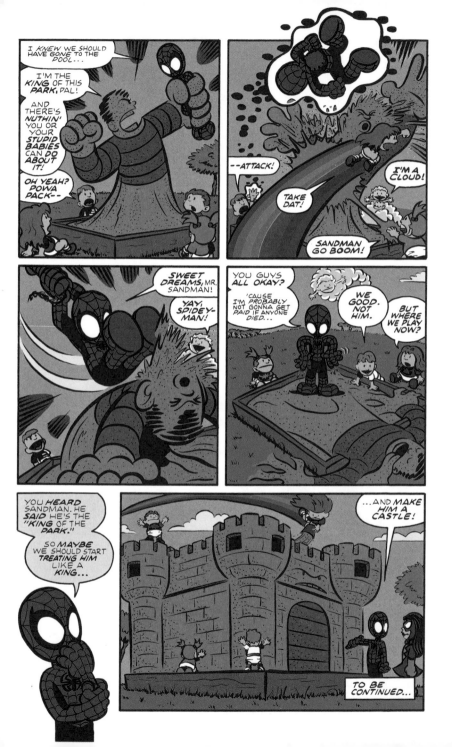

A MINI MARVELS EVENT IN FOUR PARTS
CIVIL WARDS
PART III "WHOSE SLIDE ARE YOU ON?"

Written by MARC SUMERAK   Illustrated by CHRIS GIARRUSSO
Colored by JACOB CHABOT

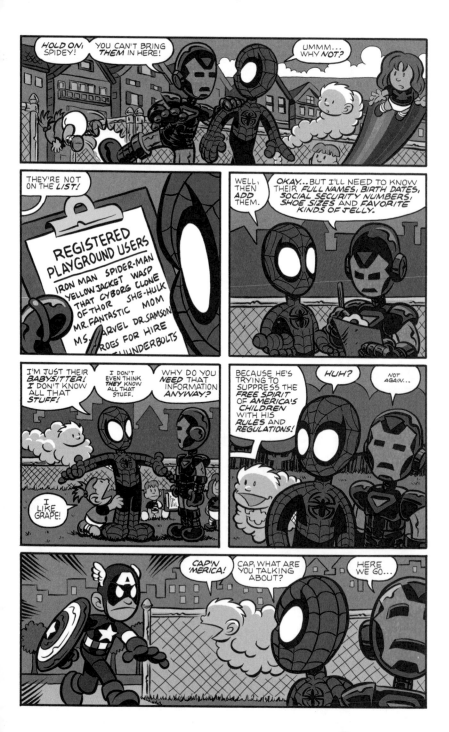

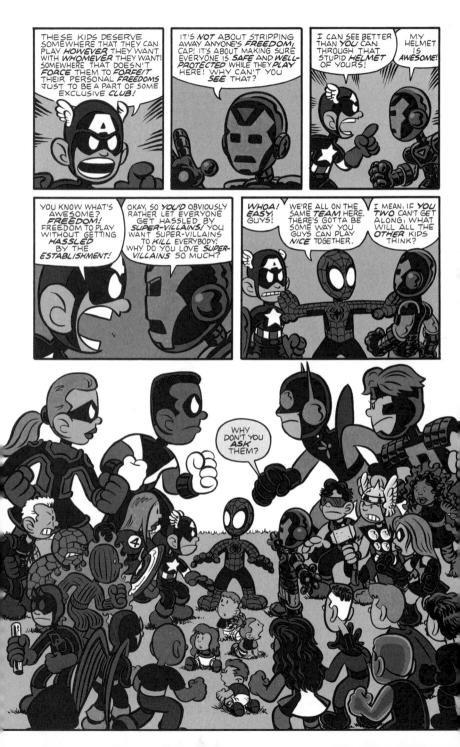

TO BE CONTINUED...

A MINI MARVELS EVENT IN FOUR PARTS

CIVIL WARDS

PART IV "THE FINAL PART"

Written by MARC SUMERAK   Co-written and illustrated by CHRIS GIARRUSSO

ZZZZZ...

... SO OTHER THAN A RUN-IN WITH *SANDMAN* AND ACCIDENTALLY STUMBLING INTO THE *SUPER HERO CIVIL WAR,* I'D SAY IT WAS A PRETTY NORMAL DAY.

"NORMAL" BEING A *RELATIVE* TERM FOR ME...

WELL, IT *SOUNDS* LIKE YOU DEFINITELY *EARNED YOUR PAY,* YOUNG MAN.

THANKS, MR. POWER...

... BUT KNOWING I'VE MADE A *POSITIVE IMPACT* ON THE LIVES OF SOME *UP-AND-COMING YOUNG HEROES* IS *FAR MORE REWARDING* THAN--

--TEN DOLLARS?

I PUT UP WITH THOSE STUPID, BRAINLESS, HYPERACTIVE LITTLE MONSTERS ALL DAY LONG FOR A MEASLY TEN BUCKS?!! WHAT DECADE DO YOU THINK THIS IS?!! YOU ARE THE STINGIEST PEOPLE ALIVE!!!

ER... THAT IS...

... ARE WE STILL ON FOR TOMORROW?

NO!

SO **CLOSE!** I'VE BEEN TRYING FOR **DAYS,** BUT I CAN'T BEAT THIS STUPID **LEVEL BOSS!**

I MEAN, HOW CAN I BE EXPECTED TO DELIVER MY **PAPER ROUTE** FOR THE **DAILY BUGLE** WHEN I'M CONSTANTLY BEING PUMMELED BY THE **AGONY OF DEFEAT?**

COME ON, NOW, SPIDEY... THE EIGHTY-THIRD TIME'S A CHARM...!

PARKERRR!

WHUH-OH. LOOKS LIKE I'VE GOT ANOTHER **KIND** OF BOSS ON MY CASE...

MR. JAMESON? WHAT'S UP?

YOU'VE BEEN **SLACKING,** PARKER! AND I **HATE** SLACKING! BUT INSTEAD OF **FIRING** YOU...

... I'M GONNA MAKE YOU WORK WITH **THESE TWO** TO GET YOU BACK ON **TRACK!**

HI, I'M **ANGEL!**

AND I'M **BOBBY!** WE'RE **BIG FANS!**

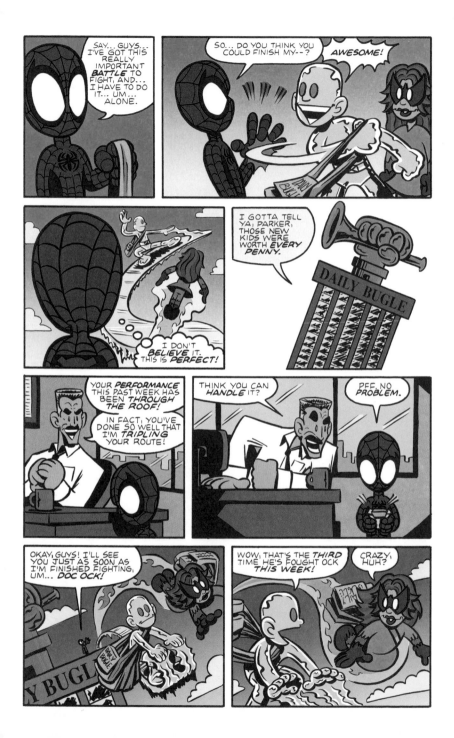

THE END.

WE know him as **STAN LEE** -- father of the Marvel Universe! But the **MINI MARVELS** know him as...

PRINCIPAL STANLEY

written & illustrated by **CHRIS GIARRUSSO**

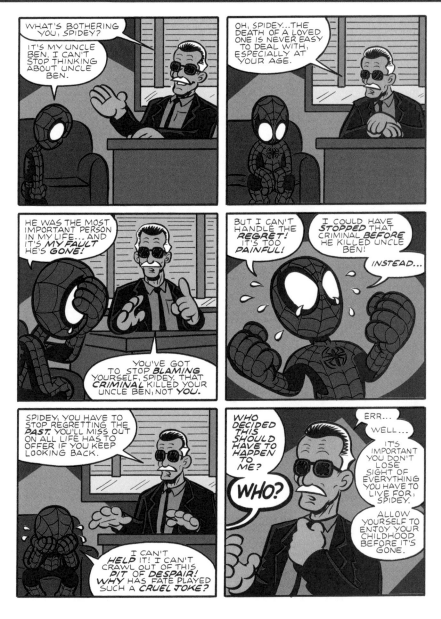

THE END.

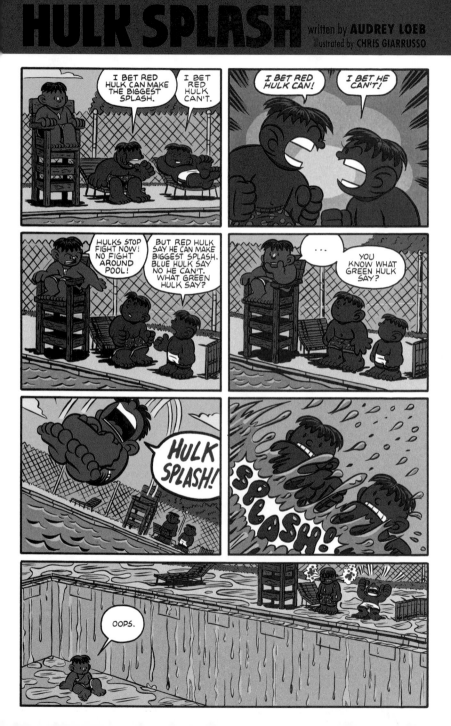

HULK ZOO

written by **AUDREY LOEB**
illustrated by **CHRIS GIARRUSSO**

HULK WEB

written by **AUDREY LOEB**
illustrated by **CHRIS GIARRUSSO**

WELCOME BACK THOR

written & illustrated by **CHRIS GIARRUSSO**

THE END.

HAWKEYE AND THE BEANSTALK

written & illustrated by **CHRIS GIARRUSSO**

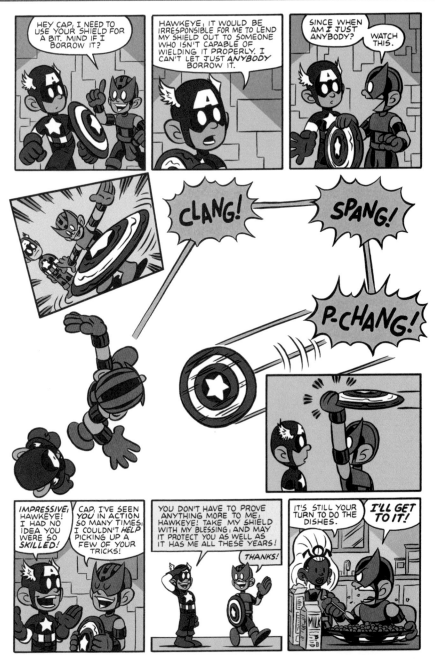

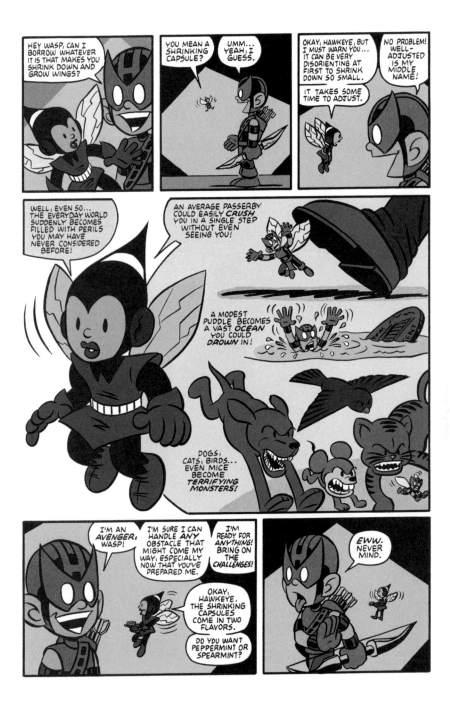

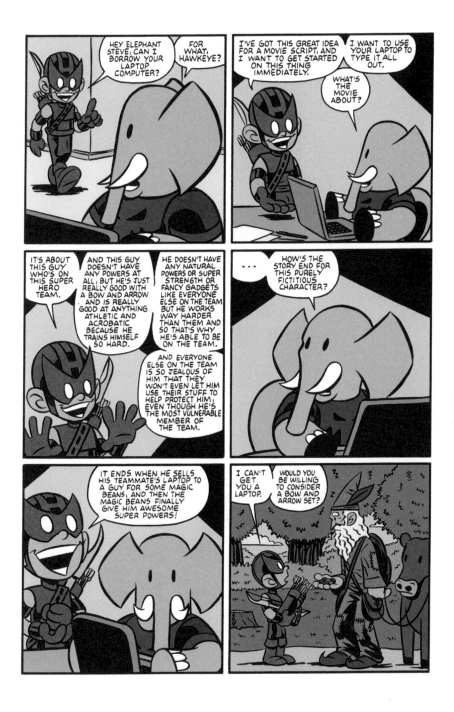

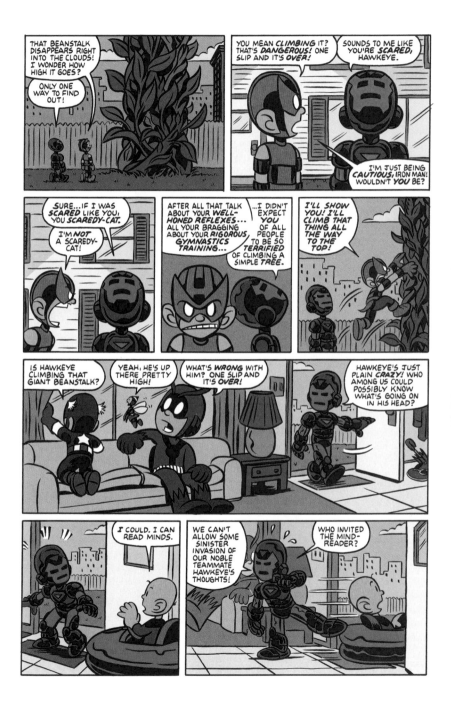

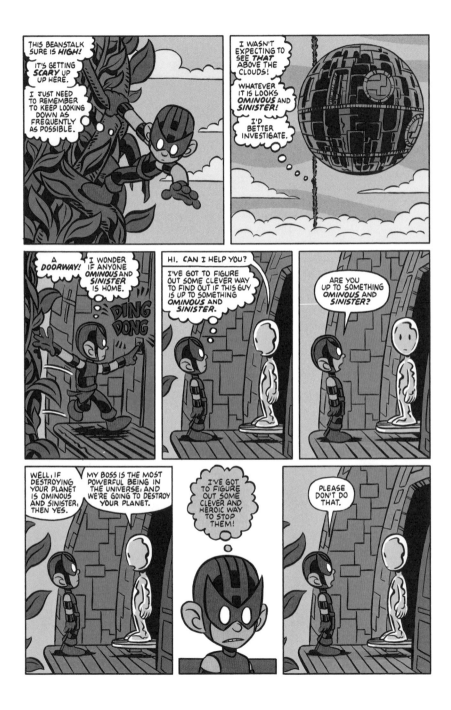

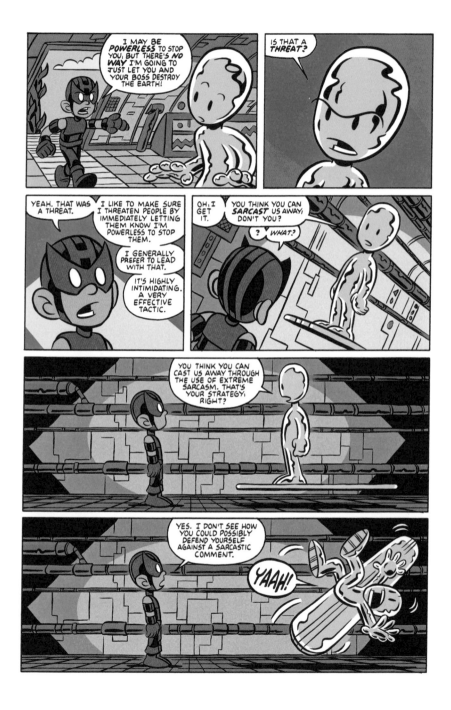

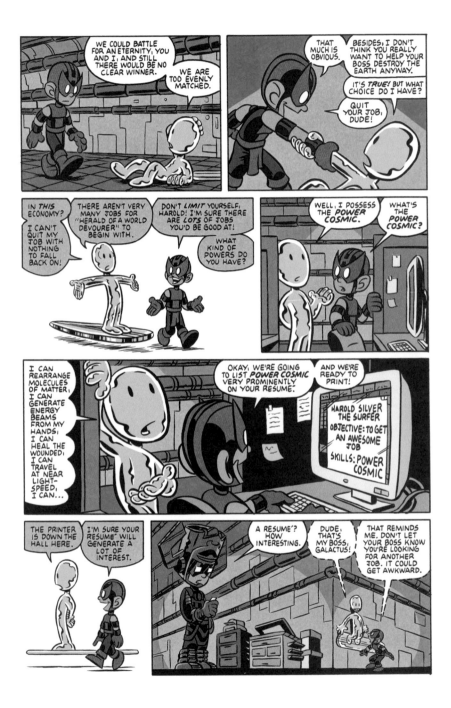

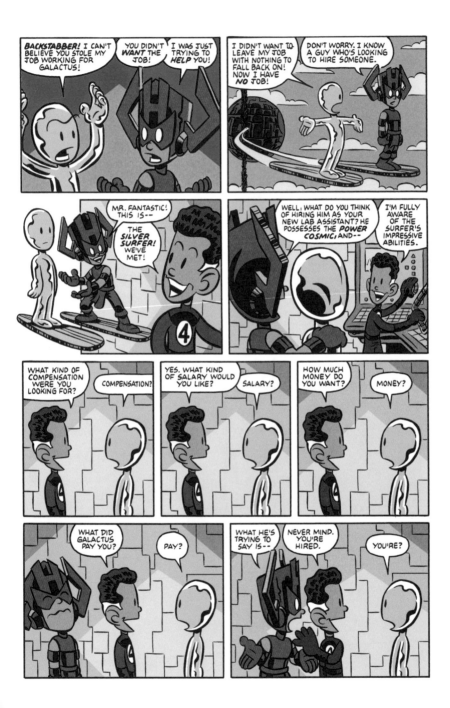

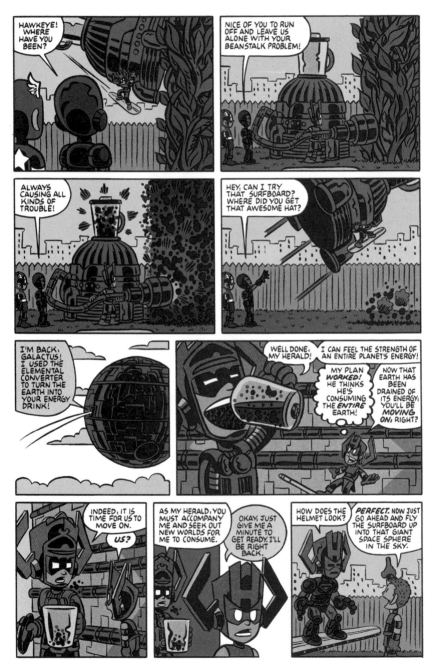

THE END.

THE COUCH

written & illustrated by **CHRIS GIARRUSSO**

THE FRENCH BREAD

written & illustrated by **CHRIS GIARRUSSO**

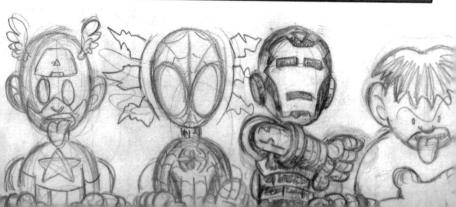

MINI MARVEL CLASSICS

written & illustrated by **CHRIS GIARRUSSO**

XAVIER, HOW CAN YOU SIT HERE AND PLAY A FRIENDLY GAME OF CHESS WITH MAGNETO?

HAVE YOU FORGOTTEN HOW HE, SABRETOOTH, MYSTIQUE, AND TOAD TRIED TO KILL US?

HEY, WOLVERINE! IT'S YOUR TURN!

WHAT DID I MISS, SABRETOOTH?

MYSTIQUE HAS "UNO" AND TOAD JUST PUT DOWN A "DRAW FOUR."

THIS IS OUR TRAINING FACILITY, THE DANGER ROOM. WITH THE LATEST ADVANCES IN VIRTUAL TECHNOLOGY...

...OUR HOLOGRAPHIC ENVIRONMENTS OFFER REALISTIC BATTLE SCENARIOS RANGING FROM THE PREHISTORIC WILDS OF THE SAVAGE LAND...

...TO THE SHI'AR GALAXY IN THE FAR OFF REACHES OF OUTER SPACE...

...BUT ALL THESE GUYS EVER DO IN THERE IS PLAY BASKETBALL!

I WANNA EAT YOUR BRAINS.

I WANNA EAT YOUR BRAINS.

I WANNA EAT YOUR BRAINS.

JUST GIVE HIM A CHEESEBURGER.

ONLY A HUNDRED PUSH-UPS? CAPTAIN AMERICA CAN DO THREE HUNDRED PUSH-UPS!

AN A-MINUS? CAPTAIN AMERICA GOT AN A-PLUS ON THAT TEST!

CAPTAIN AMERICA DOESN'T EAT SUGAR PUFFS. CAPTAIN AMERICA ONLY EATS SUGAR BITES!

CAPTAIN AMERICA DOESN'T HAVE A LOUD-MOUTHED GIRL ALWAYS CRITICIZING EVERYTHING HE DOES!

YOU SHOULDN'T ALWAYS COMPARE YOURSELF TO CAPTAIN AMERICA.